ANGEL NUMBERS

111 2 8 999 4 22 6 33 7

LOM ART

Illustrated by
Anjali Singh

Edited by Jocelyn Norbury

Written by Imogen Currell-Williams,
Bryony Davies and Jocelyn Norbury

Designed by Jade Moore
and Moesha Kellaway

Cover designed by Angie Allison

Editorial consultancy by MaKayla McRae

W www.mombooks.com/lom   f Michael O'Mara Books   𝕏 @OMaraBooks   o @lomart.books

First published in Great Britain in 2025 by LOM ART,
an imprint of Michael O'Mara Books Limited,
9 Lion Yard, Tremadoc Road, London SW4 7NQ

A CIP catalogue record for this book is available from the British Library.

ISBN: 978-1-915751-20-1

1 3 5 7 9 10 8 6 4 2

This book was printed in China.

FSC
www.fsc.org
MIX
Paper | Supporting
responsible forestry
FSC® C020056

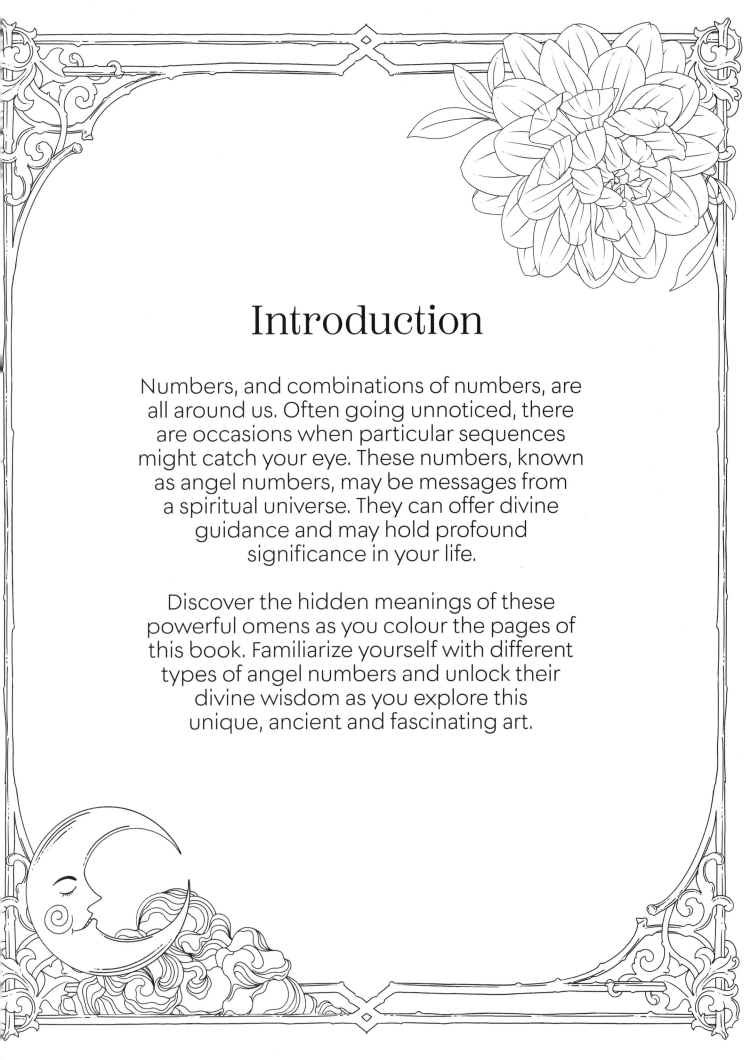

Introduction

Numbers, and combinations of numbers, are all around us. Often going unnoticed, there are occasions when particular sequences might catch your eye. These numbers, known as angel numbers, may be messages from a spiritual universe. They can offer divine guidance and may hold profound significance in your life.

Discover the hidden meanings of these powerful omens as you colour the pages of this book. Familiarize yourself with different types of angel numbers and unlock their divine wisdom as you explore this unique, ancient and fascinating art.

Angel Numbers

111

818

123

222

444

1234

369

555

333

Angel numbers are sequences of numbers that are believed to carry special spiritual significance and messages from the divine realm. These numbers often appear repeatedly in everyday life and each has a specific meaning, providing guidance, reassurance, or a call to action.

777

888

1144

Angel number 101

Just as the tiger, the 'King of the Jungle', possesses ferocity and abundant lifeforce, angel number 101 signifies that you are surrounded by great potential. This number is an omen for you to harness it.

Change and new experiences are the key to growth, and like the tiger, who is swaggeringly unafraid of predators, you should aim to tackle opportunities head-on, no matter how daunting they seem.

An extraordinary life will inevitably lead you on a path to self-discovery. In return for pursuing your goals fearlessly, you are offered the opportunity for spiritual growth and fulfilment, the ultimate aim for all existence.

Angel number 111

Representing opportunity, good luck
and achievement, angel number 111
celebrates individuality and signals
a fresh start on the horizon.

A powerful combination of the number 1
(which denotes intuition, independence
and individual power) and master number 11
(signifying the discovery of a higher purpose),
this number offers a clean sheet on which you
are able to write the story of your life as you
wish. Take a deep breath, believe in yourself
and the wisdom of your spirit guide, and
manifest your dreams intentionally.

Angel number 123

It is time to move forward with your life. The angel number 123 is an encouraging sign from the universe that good things are imminent, and you should embrace the natural changes that come your way.

This number is a signpost showing it is time to embrace the positive energy around you and use it as your guiding force, showing you the way through the treacherous mountains along the path of success. Go towards the Sun. Let go of fear and self-doubt – take inspiration from the mountain goat, who is surefooted through difficult terrain.

Cacti and succulents signify resilience. They adapt and flourish in tough environments. Relinquish your worries and take steps forward along your chosen path. Angel number 123 reassures you that the universe is on your side.

Angel number 222

A peaceful symbol of balanced and
harmonious relationships, angel number
222 encourages you to focus your energy
on strengthening existing partnerships.
Harmony roses and peonies symbolize
equilibrium. This angel number
draws attention to areas in your
life that are imbalanced.

In the natural world, the cycle of life
relies on all elements working together.
Similarly, if your relationships feel off-
kilter, this number reminds you that you
can shift interpersonal dynamics through
communication and compromise.

Angel number 234

Angel number 234 is a powerful message from the universe, symbolizing growth, balance, and trusting the process. The sequence combines the energies of 2, 3, and 4, representing harmony, creativity, and stability.

When you encounter this number, remember to embrace the natural timing and rhythm of your journey, instead of rushing to reach your final destination. Like the seasons, all of life's transitions are inevitable and important in their own right. By maintaining a positive, patient mindset you will manifest your desires.

Angel number 234 reassures you that your efforts are supported by divine forces, urging you to keep moving forward with unwavering faith and confidence.

Angel number 333

A beautiful china cup sits atop a pile of books that are embossed with the number 333. If you find yourself coming into contact with this number, it is time to embrace personal development. Turn your plans into actions – be creative and express yourself. Take up your notebook and pens and give voice to your inner feelings.

The power of the lucky number 3 is magnified threefold in this angel number. This good fortune and growth is represented by the plants and flowers, especially the money plant, framing this scene. It's a time for growth: perhaps you might be the one to expand, or you could help others to. Full-heartedly invest your best efforts to reach ideal outcomes. The sky's the limit! This advancement could be spiritual, personal or financial: however it manifests, if you are channelling your energy and love, your desires will flourish. Embrace the empowerment the universe is offering.

Angel number 369

A powerful message from the universe, angel number 369 conveys that your dreams are within reach. Number 3 is associated with self-expression and creativity, while number 6 signifies home and gratitude. Combined with the spiritual enlightenment that the number 9 represents, this angel number is a sign that you have the power to change your life.

When these three numbers appear together, your creative energy and spiritual growth are in perfect harmony, enabling you to manifest your future and bring it to reality.

Angel number 411

A number often used as a shorthand way of sending a message, 411 carries a message of guidance from the universe. It indicates that you should focus on your personal and spiritual growth, assuring you that positive developments are on the horizon. The number 4 symbolizes hard work, practicality, and a 'slow and steady' approach to building a solid foundation, while the number 1 signifies new beginnings and leadership.

In combination, 411 suggests that the universe is urging you to take proactive steps toward your goals, trusting that your efforts will lead to success. Remain patient and persistent, as your dedication will yield long-term benefits.

Angel number 444

An angel number with protection and support as its central message, a regular sighting of 444 is a sign that you are in the hands of a spiritual guide with your best interests at heart. As loyal and unwavering as 'man's best friend', your guardian offers protection and encouragement, steering you compass-like along the correct course.

Just as irises and snapdragons represent hope and positivity in the face of adversity, angel number 444 also offers an optimistic outlook. Although challenges will inevitably present themselves as you travel life's path, do not be discouraged - instead, focus on how the reward of achievement will outweigh any hardship.

The warmth and light from the Sun's rays offers a reminder that you are not alone. There is support on hand to help you through difficult times.

Angel number 511

Angel number 511 signifies new beginnings, personal freedom, and transformation. In isolation, the number 5 symbolizes adventure, urging you to step out of your comfort zone and explore new possibilities. The double 1 amplifies the energy of independence and creation, signalling that you are the architect of your reality.

With exciting opportunities on the horizon, you should act with courage and enthusiasm. In order to embrace opportunity when it comes knocking, trust change. No matter how unsettling, leaning into the unknown will lead to personal growth and fulfilment, allowing you to embark on a new, transformative chapter in your journey.

Angel number 555

As a powerful harbinger of transformation and fresh starts, this number has much in common with the fleeting beauty of cherry blossoms in the spring. Just as these flowers bloom briefly but brilliantly, the appearance of 555 suggests that significant changes are on the horizon and, with them, the opportunity for swift renewal and growth.

Angel number 555 encourages you to make peace with times of transition, trusting that it will lead to a brighter, more fulfilling path. The cherry blossom's delicate petals remind you to appreciate the present moment, as change is inevitable and necessary.

Just as the blossoms fall to make way for new growth, 555 signals that it's time to let go of old patterns and make way for fruitful, prosperous seasons ahead.

Angel number 606

Angel number 606 is perfectly balanced, indicating that you have control over decisions that impact your life. With this number in your realm, you can solve problems and make changes with confidence and reassurance.

The number 0 is bold and fearless, encouraging you to use your initiative and make choices that could otherwise feel overwhelming. Number 6 is a softer number, reminding you to be kind to yourself and to remember that things are going to improve soon. With the protection of these numbers, you are reconnected to your empowerment.

The tiny mosaic fragments delicately pieced together allude to this angel number's ability to help with problem-solving. At the same time, the symmetry of this image reflects the palindrome number and the balance this angel number can instill.

Angel number 666

If you encounter the angel number 666, it is likely you are experiencing a time of imbalance in your life. Some people fear the number, but as it is related to the core numerology of 6, it can bring love, compassion and healing. Therefore any imbalance you are sensing can be reconciled with this healing intention.

Flames lick at the numbers, but far from being a force for destruction, the fire has a cleansing and restoring power. Fireflies light up the darkness, promising to guide you and provide illumination in times of uncertainty. Luna moths, symbols of spiritual guidance, flutter in the night sky, drawn to the fire's light.

Angel number 777

Get ready. Something wonderful is about to happen! If you encounter the angel number 777 it means luck is coming your way. This could be a spiritual awakening bringing a sense of completeness, or the manifestation of something you have been waiting for. Here, the angel number is shown on playing cards, emphasizing the great things approaching. Success is also portrayed through the lucky charms on the bracelet, and the alliums, which symbolize good fortune.

Circular rings and bracelets represent completeness. This angel number will lead to healing and truth. With integrity and transparency comes motivation and action, so take heed.

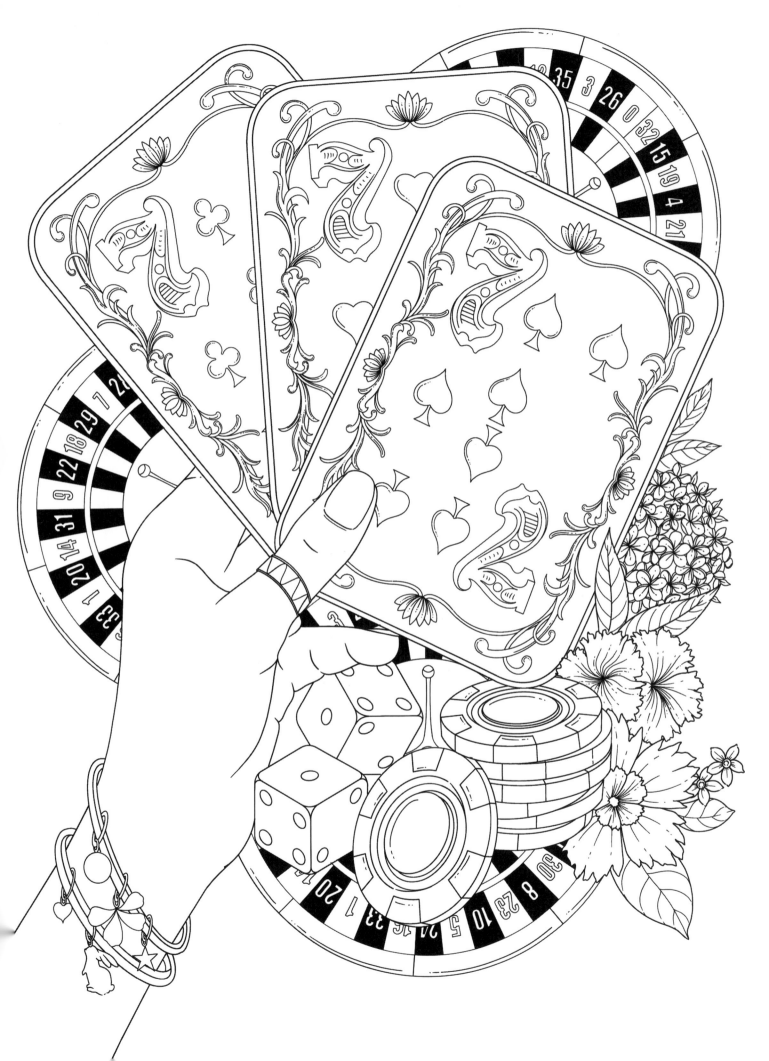

Angel number 818

Take this number as a sign from your angels that positive change is on the horizon. The dawn Sun is rising, bringing with it a new day and a fresh perspective, abundant with energy and spirit.

Just as the angel number 818 represents new beginnings, so do the flowers in bloom, symbolizing rebirth while opening themselves up to the Sun to absorb the light. You too must open yourself to the world around you, soaking up resourceful energy and harnessing its power.

8 is one of the most divine numbers. Visually similar to the symbol for infinity, it connects you to the spiritual universe and allows you to hone in on your own infinite growth.

Angel number 888

The number 8 is replete with positive associations, so it is no surprise that angel number 888 is seen as a gateway to good fortune. If you find this number jumping out at you, take it as a reminder to be open to the gifts that life has to offer. Wealth and success are in your future, and this is a sign that you are on the right path to receive your destiny.

The bounty that awaits is represented by loaded grapevines. A traditional symbol of abundance, they are accompanied by ripe pomegranates. This is a literal depiction of the 'fruits of your labour' and a reinforcement of the idea that good times are coming, in quantity. Bluebirds, associated with hope and positivity, offer up assurances that happiness is on its way. Meanwhile, peonies indicate that material wealth will play a key role in your joy.

Those who manifest this number can prepare themselves for the sweet rewards of their hard work.

Angel number 911

If you come across angel number 911, be prepared for monumental change. Number 9 is the final angel number, which means that a chapter is coming to a close. But don't be alarmed; when one door closes, another opens. The next chapter presents you with an opportunity for growth, courage and enlightenment.

The number 911 is often used in emergency situations, so be aware of any red flags. Prepare to make bold decisions to prevent negative energies entering your realm. Just like a wordly cat, use your intuition when responding. As long as you are true to yourself you will be able to navigate whatever comes your way.

Angel number 999

Now is an opportune time to celebrate completion. The master number 999 demonstrates closure and reflection on something well done. Here the three 9s emanate from a common centre, mimicking the ancient Celtic symbol called the triskelion. It contains three spirals symbolizing the cycles of birth, life and death. These three processes remind us to trust in the divine timing of our lives. New beginnings follow endings.

As an important matter comes to a conclusion, you can reflect upon what has been achieved, or has come to fruition. The power of reflection is embodied by dragonflies, which are a symbol associated with emotional maturity and self-realization.

Angel number 1234

Ready, set, go! Angel number 1234 is a hugely optimistic sign that you should prepare yourself to receive good news and welcome positive influence into your life. As succulents are thought to attract abundance, so this number is a magnet for good fortune.

Along with gathering energy from the Sun, succulents store water, allowing them to survive and even thrive over dry stretches. Perhaps you have experienced a period of uncertainty or unhappiness? This number could be an omen that difficult times are drawing to a close. The universe is preparing you for an era of spiritual affluence. Let the good times roll!

Angel number 1144

Angel number 1144 denotes that the universe is reminding you to practise gratitude. In return, you will be showered with abundance and prosperity. To employ thankfulness, you need to be open to love and light, letting it into your world so that you can reflect it back to others.

Knots are a symbol of abundance. In this image, the angel number 1144 is formed from silky, knotted ribbon. Flowers, and sunflowers in particular, are renowned for their association with gratitude. The number 1 welcomes new intentions, while number 4 encourages you to ground yourself and cultivate positive processes. The double 1 and double 4 make this number all the more energized and powerful, so be sure to harness this passion and project it into your sphere.

Angel number 2244

Angel number 2244 is a message of encouragement. Just as a compass will guide you in the right direction, seeing the number 2244 reminds you that you have the power and ability to achieve your goals. The combination of the numbers 2 and 4 are here sending a clear message that action is needed to build security and solidify relationships.

Ensure you maintain balance and stability to help you keep on an even trajectory, and know that with the energy of this angel number, you have the power to create the opportunities and life you want for yourself. Just like the animals in this image, be guided by your intuition and you will take the right path.

1010

2222

1331

Mirror
Numbers

0909

2020

0000

1111

Mirror numbers, or mirror hours, occur when the clock shows duplicate numbers. It is thought that these numbers point to a divine message, their unique meaning determined by the specific combination of numbers. They often relate to your deepest desires or emotions.

1212

Mirror number 0000

The number 0000 signifies boundless potential. Here, four interlinked Os each contain an element which characterize this promise. Dandelion seeds are being blown through the air, exemplifying freedom. A rabbit evokes rebirth and new beginnings. Climbing vines signify growth, and a butterfly, which has transformed from a caterpillar, illustrates the ability to make a completely fresh start.

To encounter the angel number 0000 is to be given a cosmic invitation to believe in the divine timing of new possibilities. Remember to be gentle on yourself: instead of being your harshest critic it is much more productive to accept your uniqueness and harness its power through positivity. The universe is telling you that you can create magic in your life.

Mirror number 1010

When the number 1010 frequently appears, you should take it as a sign to follow your intuition and stay true to yourself. Dive deeply into your pool of self-knowledge and allow yourself to be led by instinct. Just as the noble, intelligent whale navigates treacherous waters using its inner voice, so should you follow your truth.

The universe offers boundless opportunities for those who can tap into their sense of spiritual direction and who practise courage enough to explore this bold new frontier. Mirror number 1010 suggests you are ready to take this step, even if you feel nervous doing so.

Mirror number 1111

The dragon is a protector, symbolizing good luck, fortune and prosperity. It embraces the meaning of the angel number 1111, which is telling you that everything is in alignment. You are on the right track, with the dragon and the universe as your protectors.

Perhaps you have a hunch about something: if you see 1111 now is your time of power. You should seize that opportunity, set your intentions and manifest heartfelt dreams. It is the right time to act and remain empowered.

The number 1 itself is associated with new beginnings, with the commencement of journeys, creativity and leadership. When repeated four times in a row, these qualities are magnified, so take this opportunity to connect to yourself on an elevated level.

Mirror number 1212

If you notice the clock at 12:12 it could signify that your life choices have fallen out of time with your intended spiritual path. A frequent sighting of this number can be interpreted as the universe nudging you gently back on track, encouraging to retreat and reassess your direction.

On a positive note, assessing your choices in this way may simply offer reassurance that you are heading in the right direction and the confirmation that your plans will come to fruition if you continue along your current path.

Either way, this number asks you to look within yourself. What is working in your favour? What isn't? Be honest with yourself.

Mirror number 1331

Angel number 1331 carries a powerful message of growth and community. This number signifies that you are surrounded by positive energies and support, encouraging you to pursue your goals with confidence. The presence of the number 1 in the sequence emphasizes new beginnings, urging you to take initiative as you chase your dreams. The number 3, appearing twice, amplifies the message of communication and self-expression.

Highlighting the importance of collaboration and connection with others, noticing 1331 suggests that your expansion and success are linked to the support and encouragement you receive from those around you. This number encourages you to contribute positively to your friends and loved ones, using your talents and leadership abilities to inspire and uplift others.

Mirror number 2020

From a spiritual perspective, the mirror
number 2020 carries a profound message of
transformation and awakening. It signifies a time
of great spiritual growth and expansion. When you
cross paths with this number, the divine realm
is urging you to embrace this period of
change with an open heart and mind.

In this image, the padlock represents an open
heart and the number 2020 is the key to a new
era of authenticity, honesty and self-awareness.
The flowers surrounding it are powerful symbols –
dahlias stand for transformation, blue star ferns
for self improvement and caterpillars
and butterflies signify renewal.

Mirror number 2222

Like the wolf, a symbol of wisdom and guidance, mirror number 2222 encourages you to keep faith in the divine forces that are guiding you. The birds, with their innate homing instinct, trust their intuition in order to reach a place of happiness and safety. With this in mind, know that whatever the weather, you are heading in the right direction.

Although it may seem that your journey is meandering and prolonged, mirror number 2222 offers a reliable sign to trust the angels that are guiding you with your best interests at heart. With time you will arrive at your ideal destination.

Mirror number 0909

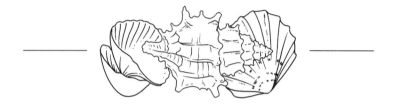

The mirror number 0909 is a sign that the best is
yet to come. You are already on your own journey
of growth, but with this number in your realm, you
can feel reassured that the spiritual universe is
looking down on you and guiding your path.

Tune into your inner voice and seek out
what no longer serves you. It is time to let go of
these things to create space for new beginnings.
This will enable you to harness your talents and
direct them into areas of your life that you want
to enhance. Number 9 represents endings
and beginnings, and although one chapter is
coming to a close the next chapter will be more
prosperous. Trust in divine timing and reap
the rewards of your journey of growth.

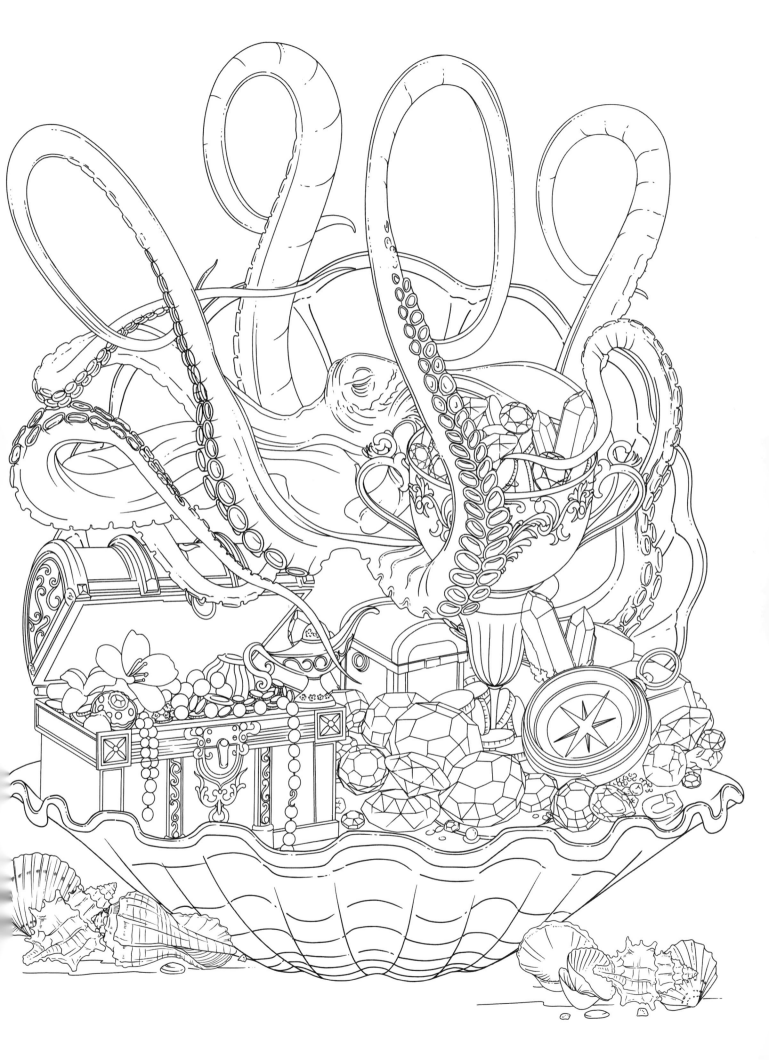

Classic
Numerology

In the ancient practice of numerology, all numbers possess a specific energy that can offer insight into a person's individual characteristics. By understanding our unique numerical code we can gain a greater understanding of who we are, where we're going and what our purpose is.

Number 0

The number 0 represents the never-ending cycle of life. Change is ahead, but for now, trust in the divine timing beyond your control. You have the power to make your dreams a reality. Even when you hit a low point, the cycle will eventually return you to a high peak. You can manifest your own changes, if you keep moving forwards with faith in your infinite cycles - just as the 0 has no beginning or end, so your possibilities are endless.

Koi carp swim calmly and peacefully, their beautiful tails fanning out. Yet hidden beneath this calm demeanour is their perseverance and strength of character. If the universe is showing you the number 0 do not be disheartened by life's challenges. You may feel void or empty, like the blankness of 0, but your time will come.

Number 1

As peacocks grow from small brown chicks to
magnificently coloured birds, so too should you
embrace the opportunity to expand and evolve.
The number 1 represents new beginnings and a
chance for you to shine. Have the confidence
to display your beauty to the world.

As the Sun rises on a new day, the number 1
radiates its light on the world and brings with it
new hope and the chance to take on life afresh.
Light creates new life and bestows the
energy to start on your journey.

Here, a border of tulips symbolizes the
opportunities that await you. Just as bulbs
lie dormant in the earth waiting for their time
to spring to life, so can you embrace this
opportunity to develop and change.

Number 2

The number 2 is a feminine force, and should encourage you to embrace intuitive power. Similarly lotus flowers, a symbol of female power and hope, rise from muddy waters to bloom and display their magnificence and strength.

Bees demonstrate the peace and partnership of the number 2. In service to the queen bee, they work busily, exuding a feeling of calm efficiency. If you encounter this number, see it as encouragement to work as part of a team, in balance with others, in order to achieve your goals.

Entwined around this number 2 is an endless knot, which in Buddhism demonstrates balance. With no beginning or end, it can be followed round forever, displaying the balance needed to empower yourself. This endless renewal is also portrayed by peace lilies, as they flourish through the seasons.

Number 3

The powerful symbolism of the number 3 is shown by the necklace the oriole birds are holding in their beaks. The pendants show the number 3 and the triquetra, an ancient symbol with three interconnecting arc shapes.

The orioles, birds which represent the power of friendship, are working together to hold up the necklace, demonstrating the power of social connection. Together we are stronger than the sum of our parts. As a social number, 3 reminds you to make the most of your connections and friendships. Hold each other up and empower one another.

Like the passionflowers that surround the birds, the number 3 also symbolizes creativity, imagination and inspiration. Snapdragons and chrysanthemums denote creativity and optimism. If you encounter this number, let your passions fly and let your loved ones inspire you.

Number 4

Take heed if you see the number 4: you are being reminded by your ancestors that you are supported, safe and stable. As in this picture, the number 4 is rooted in the ground. It is solid and fixed, and provides a basis for you to grow.

This steady and secure base should give you the power and resources you need to reach for the stars. Aim for the heavens - this number will give you a physical, mental, emotional and spiritual foundation.

With this number in mind, take the knowledge that you are being protected and use this divine guidance in whatever way you need. The clean, straight lines of the number will give you the power to take control, root down and take care of yourself. From this solid foundation grows the tree of life.

Number 5

Make like a monkey and tap into your strong sense of curiosity. Like our mischievous primate friends, the number 5 encourages us to embrace a spirit of adventure that can quickly become overshadowed by the practicalities of everyday life. Changing your daily routine could be the simplest way to shake things up and cast off the shackles that may prevent you from living each day to the fullest.

Here, bird of paradise flowers represent adventure and the beautiful surprises that await when we follow the lead of the number 5. Embrace the twists and turns of life and learn to go with the flow.

Number 6

The number 6 is linked to the domestic sphere:
it embodies the importance of home,
shown here by the welcoming front
door and steps leading up to it.

The number offers up compassion and healing.
It provides a place of peace, rest and security –
a snug space, if you like, for a cat to curl
up and have a comfortable nap.

Beautifully scented jasmine and passionflowers
climb up the walls, filling the space with a sense
of love and safety, which is also portrayed by the
heart-shaped door knocker. The number 6
offers a place of harmony and respite. It
promises dependability and domesticity.

Number 7

The number 7 is associated with intellect, introspection, and spiritual depth. Representing a quest for knowledge, wisdom, and understanding, when this number appears you are being encouraged to explore the mysteries of life.

The number 7 symbolizes the balance between the conscious and subconscious mind. People who come across this numerological omen are inclined to delve into their inner world, exploring their subconscious to gain insights that might not be immediately apparent. This introspective nature often leads one to become highly intuitive, relying not only on their intellect but also on their gut feelings and spiritual awareness.

The energy of the number 7 encourages a thoughtful, meditative approach to life. It invites individuals to look beyond the surface, integrating intellectual understanding with the wisdom that comes from connecting with their psyche.

Number 8

Renewal and regeneration are the main facets of the number 8: as chameleons can change the colour of their skin and adapt to the conditions they experience around them, so the number 8 encourages you to make the most of the chances you are given for rebirth and metamorphosis.

Strive for success with the number 8; it is the achiever. Don't be afraid to be goal-oriented. This number symbolizes prosperity, abundance and material success so aim high, have faith in your abilities and make bold choices. The lush, vibrant and tropical background here represents the boundless energy of the number 8.

In this piece, the chameleons' tails curl together to form the number. Its symmetrical shape reminds you that accompanying this possibility for personal renaissance is a sense of balance. The universe is here to support whatever changes you feel are necessary, so make them with a boldness and braveness of heart.

Number 9

If the universe presents you with the number 9, it means a cycle is close to fulfilment. This is not the final completion. Rather, it is a transition towards your next phase of goals. Here the number 9 is set inside a coin, the circular shape of which accentuates this concept of eras - and also promises luck and good fortune.

As one circle closes, another opens. This image is supported by two facing phoenixes. Symbolic of rebirth and transformation, if you encounter the number 9, prepare for new adventures and embrace the challenges in your life as they will lead to fulfilment.

A border of lily of the valley, morning glory and zinnia flowers frames the coin. A fresh start and a new dawn, coupled with the return of happiness, are promised to you by this number.

Master Numbers

11

22

33

Since the birth of numerology, certain numbers are believed to have a turbo-charged energy, possessing incredible power and potential. These double-digit numbers harness twice the power of their single-number counterparts, and the combined sum of the digits also makes them extra special.

Master number 11

The master number 11 is a powerful symbol associated with spiritual enlightenment and awakening. Two columns rising out of a moonlit pool form the number 11, representing strength. Water, the paper boats which float upon it, and trailing moonflowers symbolize dreams. The number of strength and power emerges.

The reflection of the Moon is seen in the water, surrounded by peacefully bobbing boats and lotus flowers, denoting enlightenment. The number 11 opens up new possibilities for growth, guidance and insight, guided by the illumination of the Moon.

Dragonflies, a symbol of personal growth, remind us of master number 11's message that out of chaos can come balance, power and the mastery of one's life purpose.

Master number 22

The duality of the number 2 holds a special place in our collective unconscious. Symbolizing forces such as life and death, yin and yang, or male and female, it represents balance and harmony, as envisaged by the symmetry of this circular mandala.

The number 2 is peaceful and yet powerful, and when the number appears twice as a master number, its force is doubled. Here, classic feminine traits are displayed by the posies of flowers surrounding the mandala - peace lilies, lavender and cosmos denote tranquility, as hyacinths embody grace.

The master number 22 is often linked to balance within relationships, merging two individual's energies into one. It encourages you not only to strive for internal harmony, but also to find compromise with the forces around you.

Master number 33

As a symbol of love in its purest form, Cupid is the ideal visual representation of this most romantic of master numbers. As the Roman god of love, Cupid held the power to make visions of love a reality. Master number 33 offers an inspiring reminder to bring a little love into your world.

Just as the roses, primroses, and camellias are seen in full bloom, this number tells of the importance of a whole and open heart. Bringing with it an unrivalled sense of spiritual comfort, 33, the 'Master Teacher', will help you to shine the warm light of care and compassion on those around you.